MESSY

ACTIVITIES

and More

MESSY

ACTIVITIES
and More

VIRGINIA K. MORIN

Illustrations by David Sokoloff

CHICAGO REVIEW PRESS

Library of Congress Cataloging-in-Publication Data

Morin, Virginia K.
  Messy activities & more / Virginia K. Morin ; illustrations by
David Sokoloff. — 1st ed.
      p.   cm.
  Includes bibliographical references and index.
  ISBN 1-55652-173-1
  1. Amusements.   2. Games.   3. Family recreation.   I. Sokoloff,
David.   II. Title.   III. Title: Messy activities and more.
GV1203.M7   1993   92-41453
790. 1'922—dc20   CIP

To my son ADAM,
without whom this book would not have been possible.
I love you!
And to my husband, TIM,
for his encouragement, understanding, and support.
VKM

CONTENTS

CONTENTS

FOREWORD

Determined grown-ups often over-program their children for success. Children are told "You can do better," "Don't act silly," "That's dumb," "You're too messy," "You're too big to do that," or "That's for two-year-olds." Those of us on a fast track often allow little time for and have little patience with our children. Often we unwittingly deprive them of experiences that encompass the delightfully squishy, mushy, boisterous, noisy side of life. Yet this is the very side that, in the company of a loving other, makes children feel secure and valued and the world seem fun.

How could a child who's having her hair adorned with a crown of bubbles or her muscles admired for their strength not come to view herself as the neatest kid in town? And, finding himself the focus of a solid half hour of his favorite grown-up's time and attention, how could a child not see his world as tremendously appealing? The kind of time and attention this book addresses, however, is not for tutoring in arithmetic or practicing the piano or listening to a lecture on how we keep things neat. Rather, it is time and attention for a cotton ball snowball fight, a game of "blow me over," or a challenge of who wins the arm wrestling match.

Yet, as the author nicely implies at some times, clearly states at others (e.g. "Let her win two out of the three times"), in order to be effective, activities that are fun, spontaneous, and engaging must be carried out in a climate of adult competence and maturity.

This book recognizes the child's need to be free from making unnecessary choices. Even the questions "What would you like to do today?" or "How would you like to play it?" may feel like burdens to a child. For that matter, the kind of adult questions that ask the child to concur, to permit, or to approve are experienced by her as requests to take on or share the decision-making responsibility. Often, consciously or otherwise, they are indeed intended to be just that. They are our way of abdicating our role of grown-up. We know of the burden of a spouse whose husband or wife never makes the weekend plans, seldom buys the theater tickets, or rarely calls to make restaurant reservations. We often hear the complaint, "It's so hard" or "It feels so bad to always be asked `What do you want to do?'"

Children too sometimes need to be spared the burden of being the responsible one. Children can have true fun only if they feel safe, and children can't feel safe without clear and unambiguous ground rules.

Rule number one then is: It is the adult, not the child, who is in charge. "Be sure to maintain control over the play; don't let the child take over," Morin advises in her preface.

Rule number two is: There must be no hurts. This means there must be neither physical nor emotional hurts. No hurts means neither on the part of the child nor on the part of the grown-up. Should there be a hurt, all action stops until the hurt can be attended to and the rule reiterated.

Rule number three, and a rule that cannot be too strongly stated, is: An adult must never "use" the child for the purpose of meeting the adult's own needs! Many of us remember being tickled by an uncle-type grown-up who enjoyed watching our anguished giggle; or being squeezed and kissed by overbearing aunts or neighbors—always, we knew, for their own enjoyment, not because it was genuine fun for us. Some children are so keen to please and so subtle in the way they go about pleasing that they will never let onto you that they "would rather not play this game, thank you very much." It is up to the adult to protect those children by sensing when a child is just trying to be accommodating.

Virginia Morin's cautions about making sure the child is allowed to win shows her recognition that there are grown-ups who cannot stand to lose in competition even if their small opponent is inexperienced or naive. "Don't criticize his work," the author notes, referring to Window Wash. "The important thing here is enjoying working together." "Don't ask your child to act out your own need for cleanliness," she might have said.

In using this book there are other benefits that you may not even have considered:

Carrying out the author's suggestions can be the best form of ensuring your childrens' mental health that you will ever find. As we learn more and more about the role of child-parent bonding and attachment, we are coming to see that it is these experiences that lay the groundwork for developing self-confidence and trust in others. The activities described in this book can do just that. An adult who makes good eye contact with the child, and who smiles and conveys what fun the child can have, is doing wonders to build that child a psychologically healthy foundation. "Most importantly," writes Morin, "they [the activities] give the child a feeling of power, success, and accomplishment."

Carrying out the suggested activities will widen any child's experience of herself and the world. "Beyond TV and Nintendo™ there is a people world," she'll now be able to remind herself, "and the people in it can be fun, do love me for who I am, and can introduce me to a life I never knew could be so rich and thrilling."

Ann M. Jernberg
Clinical Director
Theraplay Institute in Chicago

PREFACE

MESSY ACTIVITIES AND MORE is about enjoyment, sharing, and spontaneity. It presents playful ways to really connect with children. It is a catalyst to the reader's own deep-down playfulness. Straightforward and easy to use, this book can be flipped through to quickly find one or more activities or to plan a whole play session.

Today's kids are often tuned into television and video games and tuned out to people. This book brings people out of their daily routine to share the pure fun and joy of play. Working parents striving to make the most of the precious time they have with their children will find it particularly appealing. Teachers, therapists, grandparents, and babysitters can depend on finding useful and valuable activity ideas here.

These play ideas are geared toward people rather than projects or objects. They foster closeness and cooperation and facilitate interaction. They are appropriate for home, classroom, and therapeutic settings, as well as for parties. The activities are grouped into eleven categories: 1. Throwing, Blowing, and Ball

Games, 2. Outside Activities, 3. Messy Activities, 4. Active Games, 5. Guessing, Surprise, and Games of Chance, 6. Body Awareness, 7. Sensory Stimulation, 8. Music, 9. Cooperation, 10. Rides, and 11. Eating. Mixing activities from different categories ensures surprise and excitement.

In my search for play ideas to use with my own child and students, I couldn't find any books that focused on simple games and ideas for immediate, sensory play. I found myself making a list of the activities I remembered from my own childhood and had learned from teachers, therapists, recreation leaders, and other mothers. I kept a record of the most effective, enjoyable experiences that required no special equipment. All those presented here can be done for little or no cost. These activities can diffuse power struggles, help kids to "lighten up," gain control, calm down, and enjoy the moment. I hope my book will be a valuable, easy-to-use reference, providing parents, teachers, and caregivers with the confidence to initiate new ways of playing with and relating to children.

Virginia K. Morin

ACKNOWLEDGMENTS

I wish to thank:

Ann M. Jernberg, director of the Theraplay Institute in Chicago, whose ideas were the catalyst for this book's conception.

Phyllis Booth, Margo Wickersham-Baur, and Larry Feldman, Theraplay therapists, for their delightful and contagious enthusiasm.

David Sokoloff for bringing the book to life with his wonderful illustrations.

Amy Teschner, my editor, for her help and encouragement.

Lyle Steele, my agent, for taking care of so many important details.

Tim Harrington, my husband, for his support, proofreading, and computer troubleshooting.

Adam Harrington, my son, for his good ideas and honest opinions.

Edward Morin, my brother, for encouraging me to write this book.

Woody Haynes, for his expert computer assistance.

All the children, especially my son, who gave me the opportunity to test the activities in this book.

HOW TO USE THIS BOOK

To plan a thirty-minute play session, choose one activity from each of five different chapters. For your last two activities, choose a calming one from Chapters Six or Seven and finish with an eating activity from Chapter Eleven. Be sure to maintain control over the play; don't let the child take over. You can also use this book as a reference to look up just one or two fun activities that will surely engage kids. For further guidance on using this book, see Ann Jernberg's foreword, where she counsels: remain in charge, no physical or emotional hurts allowed, and never "use" the child to meet your own needs.

ONE
BAT, BALANCE, BLOW
Throwing and Ball Games

1

I can't recall how many times I've heard or said, "Don't throw that ball in the house." With the games in this chapter, a child can have all the throwing, batting, and swatting his heart desires. Cotton balls, balloons, paper wads, and pillows make the activities accident free.

Ball games can be difficult for a child to master. Younger children are especially frustrated; some even give up trying though they desperately want to hit or throw like older kids they see. Children will quickly master the skills required to play the games presented in this chapter. The activities are excellent for improving eye-hand coordination and large motor skills, but, most important, they give the child a feeling of power, success, and accomplishment.

The games presented here are easy, fun, and different. Play with as few or as many participants as you like. Keep score if you desire, but it isn't necessary. Often children enjoy playing more when they don't have to worry about winning or losing. The focus of these activities is not on skill levels, scores, or doing it "right," but rather on enjoyment of one another and the physical experience. Have a ball!

COTTON BALL SNOWBALL FIGHT

Materials: cotton balls, cardboard box

Place pillows, a cardboard box, or a low table between two players or teams. Pass out about thirty cotton balls to each player. The players throw one ball at a time at the opposing person or team. Keep a lively verbal account of the action ("Oh, I just got hit in the shoulder!" "I got you on your nose!" "Boy, these snowballs are freezing!" "You missed me!") To keep score set a timer, play a song, or just call time. When the time is up the side with the fewest snowballs wins.

COTTON BALL TABLE TENNIS

Materials: cotton balls, straws

Blow a cotton ball back and forth across a table. Any kind of table will do. Keep chin just a few inches above the tabletop. Arms can be extended and held against the table's side to prevent the ball from falling off. If you keep score, let the child win at least one more game than the adult. Each time the "ball" falls off the table the person on the other side gets a point. Two children can play this game or a whole class can play across tables or desks. For groups of four, try playing doubles. For variation, use straws to blow the cotton ball.

BALLOON SOCCER

Materials: 12-inch balloon

Play soccer with a balloon. Try variations like hitting the balloon with only head and elbows or only knees and elbows.

BALLOON BASEBALL

Materials: 12-inch balloon, hollow cardboard tube

Use a large (12-inch) balloon for the ball and a hollow cardboard tube for the bat. Wrapping-paper tubes are ideal. Children can take turns batting and pitching. For a more sophisticated game, run bases made of throw pillows. A chorus of "Take Me Out to the Ball Game" goes nicely with this activity. Use lots of enthusiastic accompanying rhetoric ("Hey-Hey!" "It's a grand slam!" "Listen to the crowd roar!") If the cardboard tube gets bent with use, reinforce it with masking or duct tape.

BALLOON VOLLEYBALL

Materials: 12-inch balloon, rope or string

Play volleyball with a large (12-inch) balloon. If you want to play over a net, make one by tying rope or string between two chairs or to a doorknob and a chair. See how long you can keep the balloon in the air. To play a full-fledged game use regulation volleyball rules.

BALLOON TENNIS

Materials: 12-inch balloon, toy plastic or homemade cardboard rackets, rope or string

Use a large (12-inch) balloon for the tennis ball. Cut out rackets from thick cardboard and wrap duct tape around the handles. Toy plastic rackets can also be used. Hit the ball back and forth across the same kind of net used for Balloon Volleyball. Play a set or just see how long you can keep the balloon in the air.

TOWEL OR SHEET BALLOON BALL

Materials: 12-inch balloon, towel or sheet

Grasp the edges of the towel (for two players) or the sheet (for more than two players). Place the balloon in the middle and toss it into the air with the towel or sheet and catch it again in the towel or sheet.

ARM HOOP BASKETBALL

Materials: paper

The child crumples up sheets of paper (newspaper, tissue paper, or magazine pages). Create a basketball hoop by clasping your hands together and holding your arms out in a circle in front of you. The child throws the paper wads through the hoop you have made. For the less skillful child move the hoop to catch some of the balls that wouldn't otherwise make it into the hoop. To make the game more challenging move the hoop to different levels (low, medium, high).

TELEPHONE-BOOK BALL

Materials: paper grocery bag, old telephone book

Put a large paper grocery bag on one side of the room. Give the child last year's telephone book and have him tear out pages and crumple them up into balls. He now tosses the wads into the paper bag. To make the game more interesting move the bag further away after each toss, or hold it higher or on an angle.

PILLOW TOSS

Materials: two small pillows

Two players toss the small pillows to each other. Throw the pillows at the same time so they whiz by one another in midair. Start throwing while only a few feet apart, then step back one small step each time the pillows are caught. See how far away the players can get and still catch the pillows.

PILLOW PASS

Materials: small pillow

Pass a small pillow to one another without using hands. Use two elbows, feet, knees, or chin against chest to grasp the pillow. Get yourselves into all kinds of silly twisted positions. This game can be played with two or more.

BALL BALANCE

Materials: ball, hollow wrapping-paper tube

Give the child a hollow tube and ask her to hold it upright. Place a ball on top of the tube and tell her to walk across the room while balancing the ball on the end of the tube. Place a string on the floor for the length of the walk and let her pretend she's a star circus performer on a tightrope. If you are using a thin tube, use a small, tennis-size ball. For a larger tube try a soccer-size ball.

CHAIR-LEG RING TOSS

Materials: chair, rings

Place one chair upside down on top of another chair. The child tosses rings (you can make these out of pipe cleaners with paper wrapped around them) over the upside-down chair legs. Start out throwing three rings while standing quite close to the chair, then take a step back each time the three rings are successfully thrown.

TWO

SQUIRT, WASH, TRACE

Outside Activities

Getting kids outside and away from TV and video games is advantageous to you as well as to them. You enjoy the fresh air and the benefits of being with children whose energy is being used appropriately. Joanne F. Oppenheim, author of *Kids and Play*, recognizes that "Active play provides an acceptable way for a young child to use his natural storehouse of energy. Lacking a legitimate place for spending that energy may lead to explosive backfire. Indeed, what grownups often call 'misbehavior' is really 'misplaced' and natural behavior." Children used to release some of their pent-up energy on the long walk to and from school, but today's child often either takes a bus or is driven to school.

The activities in this chapter provide opportunities to laugh, hoot, holler, splash, squish, squirt, stamp, and jump with abandon. Many of the activities involve water and should be done on warm days. Children love to play with water and it only gets them wet, not dirty!

Although I list only one winter activity, Snow Painting, don't forget about traditional winter fun like building snow people, having snowball fights, building snow forts, sledding, going for a walk, ice-skating, snow-shoveling, making angels (lying in the snow and moving your arms and legs in the snow), writing in the snow with a stick, etc. If children are acting too wild indoors, cool air helps to modulate the impulse flow from the skin and often reduces hyperactivity.

The activities in this chapter require quite a bit of energy, so be sure you're up for a good rambunctious romp!

WATER BALLOONS

Materials: balloons, markers

Fill water balloons at the tap or outside with the hose. Let the child fill his own if he is able. You can have a water balloon game of Catch; sooner or later one will break in somebody's hands. Water balloon fights are also popular. For these, everyone fills up an arsenal of balloons and then throws them at each other. Another game involves throwing the filled balloons against a wall. The big splat can be very satisfying. Try drawing faces on the balloons with markers before you throw them.

SQUIRT

Materials: water pistols or empty detergent bottles

Fill water pistols or detergent bottles that have the soap completely rinsed out. Wear clothes you don't mind getting wet and if possible take off your shoes. Run after each other making shooting noises as you squirt your opponent. Stop for refilling whenever one person runs out of water.

CAR WASH

Materials: bucket, soap, rags, hose, stool

Kids love to wash cars. They get a real feeling of satisfaction and accomplishment from tackling such a big job. Fill your bucket with warm soapy water and give the child a rag. You can each do one side of the car. The stool is so she can get closer to the roof of the vehicle. Let her rinse the car with a hose, then share the drying. If you don't have a hose available, she can rinse it by pouring buckets of water on the car and/or using a rag with clean water.

14

PAINT WITH WATER

Materials: bucket, a large and a medium paintbrush

Fill a bucket with water and provide a few different-size brushes. Your child can paint the wall, sidewalk, fence, stairs, porch, driveway, etc. Water painting can also be done inside on newspaper, brown paper, and basement walls.

SCREEN WASH

Materials: liquid detergent, brush, hose

Do this job as a team, each of you having your own screens to wash. Lay a screen flat on the sidewalk. Hose the screen off, then squirt detergent on it. Now use the brush to wash it and make plenty of suds. When the screen is lifted there will be a square of suds on the sidewalk. Playing in the suds, rinsing with the hose, and doing an important job combine to make this an engrossing, fun activity that helps build the child's sense of competence.

WINDOW WASH

Materials: bucket, water, vinegar, rags, squeegee

If you have low windows available (basement windows are ideal), they are perfect for children to wash. Let the child mix half a cup of vinegar in a pail of warm water. You can work on the higher windows while he works on the lower ones. Show him how to wring out the rag and wipe the window with it, and how to use the squeegee. Children love to use a squeegee. He will enjoy working with the water, seeing the difference between the dirty and clean windows, and using the magical squeegee. Don't criticize his work; the important thing here is enjoying working together.

POPSICLE STICK SHAVE

Materials: Popsicle stick, can of aerosol shaving cream, mirror, dish towel, washcloth, chair

Ask the child to sit in the "barber chair." Have him hold a hand mirror so he can observe all that goes on. Wrap a dish towel around his neck, barbershop-style, and proceed to lather up his face in preparation for shaving. Now shave him with a Popsicle stick. Rinse his face off with a damp washcloth. Now it's your turn. Children can also shave each other.

FLOAT AND SINK GAME

Materials: pot, floating and sinking objects

Fill a pot half full of water. Place it on a porch or sidewalk. Ask the child to collect different small objects outdoors. Leaves, nuts, stones, paper, twigs, and flowers are perfect for this game. Take turns choosing and dropping an object into the water. As the objects are tested, separate them into sink and float piles. Try mixing up the objects and see if the child remembers which ones sink and which ones float.

SEED SPIT

Materials: watermelon, paper cup

Take watermelon slices outside; eat them and save your seeds in a paper cup for a seed-spitting game. Take turns spitting one seed at a time as far as you can. Use the lines on a sidewalk for easy measurement. Children really get into this game because spitting anything is usually verboten. For a happy ending to this game, let the child win. This can also be done indoors in the basement or room of your choice.

JUMP OVER THE RIVER

Materials: two pieces of string

Place two pieces of string on the ground to create a narrow (two-inch-wide) "river." Each time the child jumps over the river move one of the pieces to make the river wider. See how far she can jump. Make sure you allow plenty of room for running before the jump and for landing.

BODY PAINTING

Materials: pail, no-tears shampoo, water, food coloring, soft paintbrush, mirror, hose

Dressed in bathing suits, bring your materials outside. In a pail, mix a capful of no-tears shampoo with water and a few drops of food coloring. Mix three or four colors in separate pails or add another color to the original pail as you paint the child's body. Paint her body with soft paintbrushes. Have her stand in front of the mirror so she can observe her transformation. Now it's your turn to let her paint you. Take turns hosing each other off or pouring a bucket of lukewarm rinse water over one another. You'll be squeaky clean at the end of this delightful activity.

LEAPFROG

Crouch down on all fours and take turns hopping over one another. See how many hops it takes to go twenty or thirty feet.

BODY TRACE

Materials: chalk

Have the child lie on the sidewalk. Tell him to get into a comfortable position. He doesn't have to be flat on his back or straight. Knees and elbows bent make interesting action pictures. Trace his figure on the sidewalk with the chalk. Let him draw in his face, hair, and clothes. Now let him trace you. Children can also trace each other. This can also be done indoors with chalk on a basement floor, or, as described in Chapter Six, the child can be traced on paper.

FEET TRACE

Materials: paper, pencil, crayons

Place two 8 1/2 x 11-inch pieces of paper or one large paper on the floor. Tell the child to stand on the paper, then trace his feet with a pencil or crayon. Let him color or draw faces on the feet tracings. Let him trace your feet; then compare your feet pictures. Be sure to comment on how fast his feet are growing.

HAND TRACE

Materials: paper, pencil, crayons

This is basically the same as Feet Trace above except the child places her hands on the paper. You can do this on a table or the floor. Try doing one tracing with the fingers close together and one with the fingers separated as widely as possible.

SHADOW TRACE

Materials: chalk

On a sunny day, trace your child's shadow on the sidewalk. Let her draw in her face, hair, and clothes. Now you strike a pose and have her trace you. Try this early in the morning or late in the afternoon to take advantage of those wonderful long, thin, giant shadows.

SNOW PAINTING

Materials: empty detergent bottle, food coloring, water

The child fills a detergent bottle with water and squeezes in drops of food coloring. Take the bottle outside and squirt designs into the snow. Try using more than one bottle for color variety.

MUD HOLE

Materials: spoon or small sturdy shovel, bucket of water or hose

Wearing old clothes or a bathing suit, the child digs a hole in the dirt and then fills it with water. Let her make mud pies, cakes, pizzas, buildings, even towns. Join in the fun to show her it's all right to get dirty. You'll be surprised at how quickly and easily the mud rinses off. This is a wonderful activity for children who are afraid to get dirty.

BOX PAINTING

Materials: large cardboard appliance box, paint, brush, knife, old blanket

With all the sophisticated toys we have today, a discarded cardboard box can still provide hours of pure pleasure. Give the child some water-based paint and a large brush and let him paint the outside and inside of the box. He can make it into a movable clubhouse. Help him cut windows in the side. Use an old blanket for the door. Play a game and eat a snack inside.

HIDE-AND-SEEK

This is the famous old standby we all know and love. It is just as much fun now as when you were a kid. Set boundaries for hiding so you won't be searching all over the neighborhood.

OBSTACLE COURSE

Materials: chalk and/or three-dimensional objects

You can make an obstacle course with almost anything. It can be two-dimensional (drawn with chalk on the sidewalk or driveway) or three-dimensional, using ropes or tires to jump over, boxes to crawl through, pieces of wood to make a "ladder" to climb on or hop between, balls to throw or kick. Try using a combination of lines and shapes drawn with chalk and three-dimensional objects. Have the child create his own obstacle course or take turns creating courses. If more than one child is playing, have the children take turns creating a course for all the children to go through.

<u>THREE</u>

FOAM, PAINT, DECORATE

Messy Activities

Have you ever noticed how playing with messy things is both engrossing and calming for children? One of the reasons messiness is so enticing is because it is usually taboo. When children get the chance to manipulate and spread things around it gives them a feeling of control and a sense of their impact on the world around them.

Childrens' natural curiosity and penchant for observation will be satisfied by the activities in this chapter. They will deflate puffs of shaving cream, see the colors of the prism reflected in bubbles, feel different textures, taste different tastes, compare sizes, mix colors, and create designs. They will learn about the world and themselves while interacting with you and other children.

The ideas in this section are tactile, creative, and silly; all elements children love. Even kids afraid to get dirty will find these activities inviting and thus will be helped to overcome their fear. Cleanup is part of the fun and is quick and easy in all cases.

If children are overexcited or hyperactive, these activities will have a calming effect. If you are planning a play session with a number of activities, messy play will fit nicely toward the end of the session. Dig in!

SHAVING-CREAM DRAWING

Materials: aerosol can of shaving cream

Squirt some shaving cream onto a formica table or other suitable surface (plastic or glass). You won't have to give instructions. Once the child has gotten used to the smooth and creamy texture, take turns drawing pictures and guessing what has been drawn or create a cooperative picture by taking turns drawing parts of a face, house, or scene. You can make up a cooperative story illustrating it as you go along or have children take turns telling and illustrating a story. A few drops of food coloring can be added to the shaving cream for variation. This is a very clean messy activity! It helps kids who don't like to get dirty learn to enjoy a mess.

A POT OF BUBBLES

Materials: dish detergent, large pot, straws, towel, water

Fill a large pot with three or four squirts of dish detergent and about three inches of water. Place a towel under the pot to soak up spills and prevent the pot from slipping. Make sure the children understand the difference between blowing and sucking. Blow through a straw to make mountains of bubbles! Two people can share one pot or each child can have his own pot. Parent and child looking at each other through a mass of bubbles is a wonderful experience. Children enjoy knocking down the bubble mountains and watching the bubbles flow onto the table.

A CROWN OF BUBBLES

Materials: bubbles or shaving cream, mirror

Place a king's crown on your child's head either by scooping up bubbles made from dish detergent or by placing or squirting a crown of shaving cream around his head. The points on the crown can be made simply by pulling up the bubbles or cream.

FOOT FOAM

Materials: aerosol can of shaving cream, towel, pot, water

Squirt shaving cream onto the child's foot, then give his foot a good massage. Repeat for the other foot. Rinse the feet in a pot or plastic tub of warm water, pat them dry, and give them a little tickle. If you like, let your child do the same to your feet. Feels great!

HAND PAINTING

Materials: water-based paint sticks, water

Use a water-based "face paint" made especially for painting skin. Take turns painting each other's fingers and nails different colors or make "hand-painted" puppets by drawing a face with the lips on the thumb and index finger. Try making an alligator by using all four fingers and the thumb for the mouth, or draw a face on the palm of the hand. Draw the eyes on one of the palm lines to make the eyes close when the hand closes. Make your puppets talk to each other or put on a musical or a play! Paint washes off easily with soap and water. Washing each other's hands makes cleanup more fun.

FOOT PAINTING

Materials: water-based paint sticks

Paint each other's foot or feet. Paint each toe or toenail a different color or make foot puppets by painting a face or a whole body with a face on the bottom of the foot. Lie in front of a mirror and put on a foot puppet show!

FACE PAINTING

Materials: water-based paint sticks

Paint each other's faces with water-based "face paint." Create clowns, monsters, animals, or whatever your imaginations come up with. Add funny hats or wigs to your creations. Take pictures or draw one another to record the fun.

CORNSTARCH HAND AND FOOTPRINTS

Materials: cornstarch, cake tin, mirror or glass

Pour about one-quarter inch of cornstarch in a cake tin. Have the child feel and experience the texture of the starch, then let her make handprints on a mirror attached to a door or wall. Do the same with the child's feet. Have her lie down and walk her feet up the mirror or pick her up to assist her "walking." Compare her prints to your own. Don't forget to mention how fast her hands and feet are growing.

FINGER-PAINT PRINTS

Materials: finger paint, metal tray or cake tin, paper

Put one color of finger paint on a metal tray, cake tin, piece of formica, or plastic. After the child has drawn and experimented with the paint, have her make handprints on a large piece of paper. Now add a new color and repeat the process. Use as many colors as you like. Create a series of pictures with the child's hands only, both your hands, hands and feet, and so on. Try putting a large sheet of paper on the floor and make prints while walking on all fours! Once again, mention how much her hands and feet are growing.

FINGER LICK AND MUSTACHE

Materials: spoon, yogurt or peanut butter, raisins, whipped cream, mirror

Decorate the child's fingers with yogurt and raisins or peanut butter and raisins. Let her lick it off. Squirt canned whipped cream above the child's lip to make a mustache. Let him lick it off while watching in a mirror.

PUDDING, YOGURT, OR WHIPPED CREAM DRAWING

Materials: pudding, yogurt, or whipped cream, tray

Spoon pudding, yogurt, or whipped cream onto a tray; use it the same way you would use finger paint. Of course licking one's fingers during painting and before cleanup adds to the fun.

YARN SPIDERWEB

Materials: ball of yarn, scissors

This activity doesn't get the participants messy, it just ties up the room for a while. Give the child or children a ball of yarn. Have him unravel the yarn over chairs, table legs, handles, etc. The room will be quickly transformed by the web of yarn. The child sees what an impact he can have on the environment. Cleanup is quick and fun: cut the yarn web with scissors and the web is broken! Yarn pieces can be reused in collages. If you want to save the yarn in one piece, have the children retrace their pattern and rewind the yarn back into a ball.

BRICK, STONE, PUMPKIN, AND GOURD PAINTING

Materials: paint, brushes, objects to paint

Kids love to paint three-dimensional objects. Give them plenty of paint and brushes and let them work on newspaper where they don't have to worry about making a mess. Painted bricks or large stones can be used for doorstops or paperweights. Gourds can be used as Christmas-tree ornaments. Just tie a string around their necks.

MURAL PAINTING

Materials: pencil, eraser, acrylic paint, brushes

Paint a mural inside the garage, on a basement wall, on the wall of a stairwell, or any other place you might find appropriate. Have your child draw his picture with pencil first. Have plenty of large erasers handy. When the drawing is ready, get out the paint. Make sure the paint is thick enough so that it doesn't run. This project can take hours, days, or weeks, depending on the complexity of the picture and the attention span of the child. When the mural is completed give a little dedication party honoring the artist. He'll be so proud of his big accomplishment. A number of children can work on the mural cooperatively. Just be sure that all involved agree which space is theirs to work on and what the theme, if any, is. Avoid conflict by planning ahead!

PEANUT BUTTER BIRDFEEDERS

Materials: peanut butter, butter knife or pinecone, birdseed, piece of yarn for hanging feeder

Spread peanut butter on a tree trunk with a butter knife to attract birds during the winter months. Or try slathering a pinecone with peanut butter, then roll it in birdseed. Tie a piece of yarn around it and hang it from the branch of a tree.

WINTER INDOOR SAND SUBSTITUTES

Materials: child's inflatable pool or cake tin; cornmeal, rice, or dry cereal; spoons; containers

Fill a small inflatable swimming pool or a large cake tin with a few inches of cornmeal. Add some spoons, containers, and a funnel and you've got hours of tactile fun. Dry cereal or rice can also be used. They make wonderful sounds when poured and swished around. I'm sure you can come up with some other wonderful ideas for materials to be used in a tactile tin or pool.

<u>FOUR</u>

LEAP, TUG, CHASE
Active Games

The rambunctious games in this chapter use lots of physical energy and/or concentration. They all require total involvement and will elicit lots of laughing, silliness, and excitement. If children get a little too wild during an activity, follow it by a quieter activity from Chapters Three, Five, or Six. A few of the games involve a show of strength. Remember, the idea is to enhance the child's self-esteem, so let her win at least one more time than you do. Be sure to remark on how big and strong she's getting. Many of the activities measure how high, how far, or for how long the child can do something. Let the child know how astounded you are at her great feats.

PILLOW HOP

Materials: six to eight throw pillows, object to retrieve

Scatter six to eight small pillows on the floor. Make the spaces between the pillows wide enough for a big jump. Place an object (ball, stuffed animal, or treat) at the end of the course. Have the child hop (with one foot or two feet) from pillow to pillow, retrieve the object, and hop back. To challenge the child further, time her and have her hop the course a second or third time, recording her improvement with each practice.

PILLOW JUMP

Materials: eight to ten throw pillows

See how many pillows the child can jump over. Make a tower, adding pillows one by one after each jump. Call out each fantastic number of pillows jumped! Be sure to allow enough room to run before the jump and to land.

PILLOW BALANCE

Materials: four to six throw pillows, piece of string

Have the child walk across the room or down a hallway with one small pillow on his head; add one more pillow after each successful walk. See how many pillows he can balance on his head before they topple. Try having the child lie on the floor with legs up and the soles of his feet flat. How many pillows can he balance on his feet? Try having him balance some pillows while walking on a string as if he were walking a tightrope in a circus. Announce him as daring circus performer.

PILLOW FIGHT

Materials: two bed pillows, timer

Hold lightweight bed pillows like sacks of potatoes. Now, ready, aim, swing! Set a timer for one minute or less to make sure the "fight" doesn't get out of hand. Be sure to remove glasses, not to hit the child too hard, and to avoid the head area.

KNEE CHASE

The child crawls as fast as he can while you crawl after him. When you catch him give him a good hug and a tickle. Turn things around and let him chase, catch, hug, and tickle you.

BALL HOP RETRIEVAL

Materials: ball (soccer-size), object to retrieve

The child places a ball between her knees and tries to hold it there while hopping across a room or down a hallway. At the end of the course the child retrieves an object (a grape, a piece of candy, a stuffed animal). To add more challenge, have her try to pick up the object without the use of her hands, by using elbows, wrists, knees, feet, or teeth.

LEAPFROG

Crouch down on all fours and take turns hopping over one another. Play in a hallway, basement, or large room. See how many hops it takes to go from one end of the course to the other.

RING-AROUND-THE-ROSY

This is the traditional game of walking around in a circle holding hands and singing. Take turns changing the last line from "all fall down" to things like "all jump up," "crouch down," "lie down," "sit down," "roll around," "shake your hands," "stick out your tongue."

SNAKE SLITHER

The child pretends he's a snake crawling through your legs and arms. Try to keep him from slithering away, but let him, with some effort, free himself from your unsuccessful holds. Complain about the slippery snake getting away again. Chances are he'll be right back to be recaptured.

HIGH JUMP

Materials: hollow cardboard wrapping-paper tube, clothesline, or rope

Crouch or kneel down and hold a hollow cardboard tube out for your child to jump over. Raise the tube a bit higher each time. Be sure to allow plenty of room to run before the jump and to land. She'll want to take quite a few turns. Show your surprise at how high she can jump. If more than two are playing, hold a rope or clothesline at each end and raise it little by little.

LIMBO

Materials: hollow cardboard wrapping-paper tube, clothesline, or rope

Hold the cardboard tube up for your child to walk under. Lower the tube a tiny bit each time he successfully makes it under. Let him roll or crawl under as the tube gets really low. If more than two are playing, hold a rope or clothesline at each end and lower it little by little.

RAG TEAR

Materials: old sheet

Give the child an old sheet and let her tear it up into rags. The sound of the tearing and the power the child feels at creating something by her own brute force is enough fun by itself, but you can also use the rags to wash each other's hands and feet, a bike or trike, the car, a mirror, or the windows.

JUMP OVER THE RIVER

Materials: two pieces of string, clothesline, or rope

Place two pieces of string, clothesline, or rope on the floor to create the width of a "river." Each time the child jumps over the river move one of the pieces to make the river wider. See how far he can jump. Make sure you allow plenty of room for running before the jump and for landing or falling.

TOWER KNOCK

Materials: throw pillows or blocks

The child builds a tower with throw pillows, cardboard blocks, or blocks made of old shoe boxes. To make safe shoe-box blocks, tape the lids on securely by wrapping masking or duct tape around the box. Once your box is sturdy, hit all four corners against the floor to soften the sharp corners. Work with your child and make the blocks together or demonstrate for a group of children and let them make the blocks. You'll need about fifteen blocks to make a good tower. Once the tower is erected, the child crawls toward the tower on all fours and knocks the tower down with her head.

OBSTACLE COURSE

Materials: chalk and/or three-dimensional objects, timer

You can make an obstacle course with almost anything. It can be two-dimensional (drawn with chalk in the basement or outside) or three-dimensional, using ropes to jump with or over, large cartons or hula hoops to crawl through, pieces of wood to make a "ladder" to climb or hop between, balls to throw or kick, and so forth. Try using a combination of chalk lines and shapes with three-dimensional objects. Have the child create his own obstacle course or take turns creating courses. If more than one child is playing, have the children take turns creating a course for all the children to go through. Time yourselves to see if you finish in less time with practice.

TUG-OF-WAR

Materials: sheet or blanket

A rope slipping through the hands could cause skin burns, so use a sheet or blanket instead. Start the "war" by winking or wiggling your nose. Use lots of body language to show how hard you're trying to pull. Let the child win one or two out of three games. Don't forget to remark on how strong she's getting.

ARM WRESTLING

Both wrestlers put one elbow on a sturdy table to start an arm-wrestling match. Interlock your fingers and push against the other hand. Let the child win one or two out of three matches and remark on how strong he's becoming.

WHEELBARROW

Hold the child by his ankles, calves, or hips while he walks on his hands. Try timing yourselves to see if you get faster with practice. With a number of children, organize a wheelbarrow race.

WRESTLING

Materials: timer, damp cloth, ice water or juice

Set a timer for two minutes, go into your respective corners, say "ding, ding, ding," and come out wrestling. You can do this on a bed or on the floor. Be careful not to be too rough. Let the child pin you a few times. When the timer goes off, the round is over. Take a rest, wipe each other's brow with a damp cloth, and give each other a sip of ice water or juice. If you both feel like having more rounds, reset the timer and go for round two, three, or four. This has been traditionally a father-son game, but moms and daughters or sons enjoy this kind of roughhousing too.

FOLLOW THE LEADER

Take turns being the leader. Do somersaults, hop on one foot, stick out your tongue, walk in a crouched position, and so forth. You'll be amazed at the funny ideas kids think up. Be sure to tell them what great ideas they're coming up with.

NEWSPAPER PUNCH

Materials: old newspaper

Kneel on the floor with the child. Hold up one sheet of newspaper very taut at arms' length and over to one side of your body. Ask her to punch through the paper. The paper will break in two. The "pow" sound it makes is like a movie sound effect. She will love the feeling of power she gets from breaking through the barrier. Do this three to five times so she really gets the hang of it.

<u>FIVE</u>

WHO, WHAT, WHERE
Guessing, Surprise, and Games of Chance

hildren love surprises and suspense. The giggling anticipation of a hiding child during a game of hide-and-seek is a real joy to behold. And you will be surprised at how much anticipation you will feel while waiting to be found.

Through play, children come to experience and understand themselves and others. They also learn that taking turns can be lots of fun. It is just as much fun to hide as to seek, to be Simon as the one Simon is directing. The games in this chapter give children the chance to be on both sides of the fence, to observe how others react to them, to be the initiator and the responder. Now it's your turn!

FLOAT AND SINK GAME

Materials: small floating and sinking objects, sink or dishpan filled with water, paper or dish towel

Gather five objects that float (clothespin, plastic bottle top, thin rubber band, toothpick, ice cream stick, etc.), and five objects that sink (coin, key, paper clip, button, shell, etc.). Or let the child pick out ten small objects from around the house. Have her place each object in the water to test if it is a floater or a sinker. Lay paper towels or a dish towel on the table so she can make two piles (floaters and sinkers) with the objects when she removes them from the water.

BACK WRITING

Use your index finger to print letters on the child's back. He guesses one letter at a time as you spell out words or sentences. Sentences like "I love you" or "You are beautiful" will boost any child's self concept. Try writing sentences that describe the child like "Adam has brown hair" or "Jenny has blue eyes." Guessing names of animals, flowers, colors, relatives, and sport teams will provide you with lots of material. For variation, try writing on the palm, foot, or tummy. Writing on each other's palm can easily pass the time while waiting in the doctor's office.

HIDE-AND-SEEK

This is the famous old standby we all know and love. It is just as much fun now as when you were a kid. I remember playing this game outside as a child, but playing indoors offers a lot more creative possibilities. Children hide inside empty cabinets, suitcases, behind the shower curtain, under tables and blankets, and in closets. This game works well with a small class of preschoolers too. Take turns counting slowly to ten while covering your eyes, then say "Ready or not here I come."

HIDE-AND-SEEK FOR OBJECTS

Materials: clothespins, pencils, spoons, pennies, or hard candies

Hide five to ten or more like objects in one room while the seeker covers her eyes and counts slowly to ten. Let her know when she's getting warm, cold, or hot (near or far from the hidden object). Now switch roles and let her hide the objects from you; change rooms if possible.

ONE POTATO, TWO POTATO

This is the popular old standby hand game where you make a fist and hold it upright, the child then places her upright fist on top, then you put yours on top of hers, and so on. The rhyme "One potato, two potato, three potato, four, five potato, six potato, seven potato, more," keeps the count as each fist is placed. The last one to place a fist on top is the winner.

HOT POTATO

Materials: timer, potato

Sit on the floor facing each other or in a circle if there are more than two players. Set a timer for one minute or less and pass a potato to each other or around the circle. Whoever is holding the potato when the timer goes off gets a hug, tickle, or kiss.

PANTOMIME

Pantomime can develop a child's creativity and self-confidence. Write what is to be acted out on an index card. Have at least eight cards per game. Try acting out feelings like tired, happy, sad, scared, surprised, cold, hot, and sick. Or try different kinds of work like firefighter, mail carrier, bus driver, pianist, painter, boxer, teacher, and carpenter. Other pantomime categories could be different sports (swimming, baseball, fishing, tennis, golf, hockey, skating, and rowing), types of housework (dusting, sweeping, vacuuming, ironing, setting the table, and cooking), or ways of walking (as if you had a sore foot, were in a hurry, in a parade, very old, a model, proud of yourself, or walking a dog).

MAGNET FISHING

Materials: construction paper, scissors, stapler, string, hook magnet, pen, index cards

Cut several ten-inch-long fish out of construction paper. Put about fifteen staples close together on the body of each fish. Attach pieces of string to hook magnets; these will be your "fishing poles." Write a number on the back of each fish to correspond to instructions on numbered index cards. Make up instructions like rub your tummy, stick out your tongue, do a somersault, hop on one foot ten times, touch your toes, do ten jumping jacks, do ten twists with hands on hips, or touch your nose with your toe. If the child or children are old enough let them help cut out, staple, and number the fish, tie the string on the magnets, and make and number the instruction cards. This can be a game for a whole class, a birthday party, or just the two of you. Using different colors of construction paper can help teach colors as you comment of the color of each fish caught. This game makes following instructions fun.

HOLD STILL NOW, BOTTLE!

CLOTHESPIN DROP

Materials: clothespins, bottle or box

Drop clothespins into a bottle or a box. Try standing on a chair to make it more challenging. Count the number of pins the child gets into the container. Give her several turns so she gets a feeling of accomplishment from her improvement.

SPIN THE BOTTLE

Materials: bottle

Sit in a circle with a glass pop, water, or wine bottle in the middle of the circle. Take turns spinning the bottle. When the bottle stops, whoever the bottle is turned toward gives a hug or kiss to the bottle-turner. Then it is that person's turn to spin the bottle. Keep playing till everyone gets a hug or kiss.

UNWRAP

Materials: wrapping paper or comic-strip paper, tape, small surprise or treat

Put a small present or treat in a little box. Then wrap it in a page from the comic section or in gift wrap. Put the small package in a larger box and wrap it. Continue to put the box into larger and larger boxes. Use seven boxes and let the child have the first turn at unwrapping, you take the next turn, he the next, and so forth. He will end up with the last box with the mystery object inside.

SIX

WHO AM I?
Body Awareness

59

Many of the activities throughout this book promote body awareness, particularly the messy and sensory stimulation activities in chapters three and seven. The activities in this chapter, however, focus exclusively on how the child's body looks, feels, and works. There is a lot of experimentation in this chapter; the child changes her appearance by trying on different shoes and hats and by making faces. She also gets a good look at herself through body tracing and measuring. Specific body parts are focused on through tracing, shaking, counting, lighting, and dressing and drawing in front of a mirror. The exercises, headstand, and acrobatics give the child a feeling of control as he makes his body do what he wants it to. The blowing and sucking game gives him a feeling of power.

A child's self-awareness develops from birth. The activities in this chapter will add some fun ways to nurture that growth.

EXERCISE

Take turns making up exercises and then do them together. Give yourselves a little workout by doing ten to twenty of each exercise. Jumping jacks, sit-ups, knee bends, torso twists, push-ups, arm circles, leg raises, and aerobic exercises are a few ideas for this activity.

HEADSTAND

Materials: towel

Give the child a folded towel to put under his head. Have him remove his shoes and try standing on his head in a corner of the room. Help him balance when he needs help. Let him stabilize himself against the wall whenever he needs to. Count for as long as he stays on his head and congratulate him on his spectacular feat!

ACROBATICS

Lie on your back on the floor. Make sure there is plenty of space around you so the child can't get hurt by falling on or bumping into any furniture. Put your knees up and your hands out and ask your child to take your hands and climb onto your knees (one foot on each knee). Slowly the child should balance himself and begin to stand in a more upright position. When he feels secure enough, let go of his hands so he can stand up straight. Extending his arms from his sides like a tightrope walker can help his balance. Tell him to jump off to the side when he can no longer keep his balance. This trick requires a little practice but it's worth it.

An easier variation of this trick is the tummy balance. Lie down on your back with your knees bent and your bare feet up. Ask the child to take your hands and lie with his stomach on your feet. Hold his hands while extending your legs as far up as possible. Let go of his hands when you both feel secure enough. Bend your knees slowly to let him down.

IMITATE SOUNDS

Take turns imitating a sound the other makes. Try high-pitched and low, loud and soft, short and long. Blowing, whistling, click-ing, and humming are some examples. You can also use other parts of the body, like rubbing the soles of the feet on the floor, tapping the thighs and knees with the hands, tapping the feet and fingers, clapping the hands, or snapping the fingers.

BLOW THE MAN DOWN

Sit on the floor with your legs in front of you. Tell the child to blow at you as if she is a stormy wind in the sky. As she blows as hard as she can, you fall down on your back. Now ask her to suck as if sucking through a straw to raise you back up. As she inhales, you slowly rise. She will love the feeling of power she gets from seeing you fall down and rise up. She will invariably ask "Did I really blow you over?" You can switch places and try to blow her down but be prepared for failure. You just might not have that magic strength!

HOW MANY?

Sit down with the child and count all of his freckles, scabs, bruises, or teeth. For added humor count three eyes, two noses, one ear, or two mouths. Let him count your freckles, eyes, and noses, just as you did for him.

SHOE SWITCH

Materials: shoes, mirror

Drag out a few pairs of everybody's shoes (sandals, slippers, gym shoes, or dress shoes). Give the child Mom's and Dad's shoes to put on and walk in. Have a full-length mirror available so he can see how funny he looks in Dad's clodhoppers. As each person takes a turn, the others should watch him. Ask the child how he likes the shoes (if they're heavy, light, big, or hard to walk in). When you try the child's shoes on, make jokes about their being too big, then just stick in your toes and tiptoe in them or put them on your hands and walk on your hands and knees.

HAT SWITCH

Materials: hats, mirror

Drag out lots of hats. Try to include as many different types as possible (helmets, brimmed hats, visors, straw hats, knit hats, and dress hats). In front of a mirror, take turns putting the hats on each other. Try each hat on in many different ways—tilted to the side, back, or front, pulled way down, etc. You'll have a lot of laughs with how silly you can look in hats!

FLASHLIGHT ON BODY

Materials: flashlight, mirror

In a darkened room in front of a mirror, the child puts a flashlight in his mouth and observes his red cheeks as he puffs them out. Then he can place the flashlight under the chin so the light is caught by his mouth and the tip of his nose. After making these jack-o'-lantern faces he can shine the flashlight through his fingers and toes.

FLOPPY-TIGHT-FLOPPY

The child lies down and you kneel by her side. Tell her to pretend she is a rag doll and let her body be all loose and floppy. Slightly lift each arm and each leg off the floor and let it fall to test how relaxed she is. Now tell her to tighten up all her muscles like a toy soldier's. Feel how hard and rigid her arm and leg muscles are and comment on her great strength and body tone. Now ask her to make her body all loose and floppy again. She will become aware of her control over how her body feels and will be able to use this technique to relax herself.

FOIL FACE, ELBOW, KNEE, HAND, AND FOOT CASTS

Materials: heavy-duty aluminum foil

Cover the child's face with aluminum foil. Press lightly to conform aluminum to his face. Carefully remove the foil and hand it to him—Voilà! A silver mask! Try covering one of his elbows, knees, hands, or feet. The foot "cast" will look like a foil slipper.

BODY TRACE

Materials: brown or white wrapping paper, pencil, scissors, crayons or markers

Cut a large enough sheet from a roll of brown wrapping paper for the child to lie down on. Tell him to get into a comfortable position. He doesn't have to be flat on his back or straight. Knees and elbows bent make interesting action pictures. Trace his figure and then cut it out or let him cut it out. Provide crayons or markers so he can draw his face, hair, clothes, and shoes. Older children might want to draw their skeletons or internal organs. Hang the figure on the wall in his room. Do this at least once a year so he can see how much he's grown.

FACE TRACE

Materials: paper, pencil, scissors, paste or stapler

Place a piece of paper measuring about 17 x 20 inches on a table. Ask the child to sit down and place her cheek on the paper. Tell her how nicely shaped her forehead, nose, mouth, chin, and neck are as you trace her profile. Cut out the silhouette and paste or staple it to a light-colored paper or, if she is able, have her cut, paste, and staple it herself. A black silhouette on a white background always looks striking but other color combinations can look great too. She can color the silhouette with crayons or markers or paint. Try purple on pink, brown on orange, dark blue on light blue, and so on. If she uses paint make sure the paper is thick enough so it won't curl up.

SHADOW TRACE

Materials: light, tape, paper, pencil or crayon

Shine a light toward a wall and place the child in a position so his shadow will be cast on the wall. Tape a piece of paper large enough to fit the shadow and trace the shadow onto the paper. You will have to remind the child to stay still while you are tracing. Do your tracing as quickly as possible because he won't be able to hold a position for very long. Try tracing giant shadow hands or just the face in profile. After you trace him, let him trace you. Silhouettes can be cut out as above.

FEET TRACE

Materials: paper, pencil, crayons

Place two 8 1/2 x 11-inch pieces of paper or one large paper on the floor. Tell the child to stand on the paper, then trace his feet with a pencil or crayon. Let him color or draw faces on the feet tracings. Let him trace your feet; then compare your feet pictures. Be sure to comment on how fast his feet are growing.

HAND TRACE

Materials: paper, pencil, crayons

This is basically the same as Feet Trace above except the child places her hands on the paper. You can do this on a table or the floor. Try doing one tracing with the fingers close together and one with the fingers separated as widely as possible.

HOW BIG AND HOW HEAVY?

Materials: measuring tape, paper, pencil, mirror, scale

In front of a mirror, measure the child's height, waist, width of smile, length from shoulder to shoulder, knee to ankle, knee to waist, waist to neck, circumference of head and biceps, width from eye to eye, and span from fingertip to fingertip when arms are extended. Write all of these figures down. You could draw a picture of the child and write the measurements near the appropriate places or write them on her body-tracing picture. She will be thrilled with all these numerical details. Tell her how remarkable the numbers are while doing your measuring work. Weigh her on a scale and record her weight. Hang the paper on the wall and add new measurements as time goes by.

HOW TALL ON THE WALL?

Materials: measuring tape, ruler, pencil

Pick a spot on a wall where you can keep a running growth chart of your child. Have him stand up straight with heels against the wall, measure him, and draw a line on the wall with a pencil. Record his height and the date next to the line each time you measure him.

FINGER-TOE COUNT

Count the child's fingers and toes, pretending to count to nine, eleven, or twelve. Repeat the counting over and over, trying to get it right each time. You will be surprised how this simple game delights children.

HAND-FOOT SHAKE

This is a silly game consisting of shaking hands and feet in every possible combination. Sit on the floor facing each other and shake hands saying "How do you do?" Then cross your arms and shake both hands saying "How do you do?" to each other again. Continue by uncrossing arms and shaking both hands again, then shake one of the child's feet with your hand, then both feet, then foot to foot, and so on. Say "How do you do?" for each shake you make.

IMITATE FACES

Materials: mirror

In front of a mirror, take turns imitating the funny faces the other makes. Sticking the tongue out in different directions, widening or squinting the eyes, and contorting the mouth will give you plenty of silly combinations.

MIRROR DRAWING

Materials: mirror, paper, pencil or crayons

Sit in front of a mirror with the child and ask him to draw a picture of himself while you draw one of yourself. When you're finished show each other your pictures and comment on what a good artist he is. Now draw each other from your mirror reflections. Show each other your pictures and have a good laugh!

SEVEN

HEY! THIS FEELS GOOD!

Sensory Stimulation

In *Creative Therapy*, Veronica Sherbourne, a teacher for the National Association for Mental Health, writes, "…rolling, bouncing, swinging, playing in water, the child experiences himself as a whole…". " The sense of his wholeness, of his totality, gives the child a sense of well-being and harmoniousness. It helps to establish the child in his body. The unconscious bodily experiences precede the development of the more conscious sense of identity in the child."

A. Jean Ayres writes in her book *Sensory Integration and the Child*, "Through play the child obtains the sensory input from his body and from gravity that is essential for both motor and emotional development. The sensory input is what makes it 'fun'. One of the reasons children play is to get this input. They need lots of it while they are young, and less as adults. The more varied his play, the more it contributes to his development."

Most of the activities in this book provide the opportunity for this essential sensory input. Many of the activities in this chapter focus on touch and pressure sensations that calm or arouse the nervous system. It also includes games involving sight, hearing, smell, and taste. There is at least one game for every sense, and they're all fun!

HUG ROLL

Lie on the floor with your child and while hugging each other roll across the floor and then back to where you started. Use your arms to lift your weight off her as you roll over her. Sing a song while you are rolling like "Roll, roll, roll yourselves gently down the stream, merrily, merrily, merrily, merrily, life is but a dream."

PASS THE CHILD

With two adults, pretend to toss the child to each other. Count "one, two, three..." or unexpected numbers like "one, six, five ..." and then pass her to the other adult. Be sure she is enjoying the game and is not frightened. If she seems the least bit afraid stop the game and go on to a calmer activity.

PASS AROUND SOMETHING NICE

Sit in a circle (three or more people make this game more fun) and take turns initiating something nice to pass around the circle. A gentle rub, blow, pat, hug, kiss, or positive words are some ideas.

BACK WRITING

Use your index finger to print letters on the child's back. She guesses one letter at a time as you spell out words or sentences. Sentences like "I love you" or "You are beautiful" will boost any child's self-concept. Try writing sentences that describe the child, like "Adam has brown hair" or "Jenny has blue eyes." Guessing names of animals, flowers, colors, relatives, or sport teams will provide you with lots of material. For variation, try writing on the palm, foot, or tummy. Writing on each other's palm can easily pass the time while waiting in the doctor's office.

TICKLE TURNS

In her book *The Stress-Proof Child*, Antoinette Saunders says, "Tickling, if it is done properly, is a good way of being physical and close. It is also less threatening than other forms of touching to a child who is suspicious, for whatever reason, of physical closeness. Letting the child tickle you also gives the child the feeling that his touch makes others, especially you, feel good." Ann M. Jernberg, Director of Chicago's Theraplay Institute, cautions that children might pretend to enjoy tickling to please an adult. It's your responsibility to sense the child's true feelings. If you're not sure, it's best to follow the old adage, "When in doubt, don't."

Take turns tickling each other. Be sure to stop when the child asks you to. He might say "Again!" right after you stop but it's important for him to know that you will respect his boundaries and wishes.

HAMBURGER

Materials: two bed pillows or chair cushions

Put a bed pillow or a chair cushion on the floor and ask your child to lie on it. Tell him he's the hamburger and the pillow is the bun and you're going to put the "works" on the burger. While kneeling next to him pretend to put catsup, mustard, tomato, onions, pickles, and so forth on top of him. Use gentle rubbing and soft tickling motions as you describe each topping you are putting on. When finished, put a pillow on top of his tummy and pretend to gobble up the "burger."

TACO

Materials: blanket

This is similar to Hamburger above except the child lies on a blanket—the "tortilla"—while taco ingredients are put on. Once all the ingredients have been rubbed, slathered, plopped, and tickled on, wrap her in the blanket and pretend to gobble the taco.

BLANKET SWING

Materials: blanket

Spread a very strong blanket on the floor and ask the child to lie on it lengthwise. Be sure his head and feet are completely inside the blanket. An adult at each end of the blanket lifts two corners and gently swings him. Make up a soothing swinging song while swinging high, low, or slow.

MUTUAL HAIR COMB

Materials: comb or brush, mirror

Comb and/or brush the child's hair while she watches in a mirror. Tell her how shiny, strong, dark, light, curly, straight, and so forth her hair is while you comb or brush it. Let her comb and/or brush your hair too. This can be very relaxing or very silly depending on the participants' moods.

MUTUAL HAND MASSAGE

Materials: hand cream

Put some hand cream in your palm and spread it on one of your child's hands. Slowly massage each finger (do not pull them), his thumb, palm, sides, and back of his hand. Then repeat the massage on his other hand. When finished let him massage your hands. For variation, try massaging each other's arms as well.

MUTUAL FOOT MASSAGE

Materials: hand cream

This is the same as the hand massage above except you massage each other's feet. Massage each toe (do not pull), her sole, sides, and top of her foot. Use firm long strokes so you won't tickle her.

CHEEK-RUB GUESS

Materials: textured objects

Ask the child to sit down in a comfortable place and close his eyes. Gently rub his cheek with different textured objects. A feather, emery board, apple, teddy bear, and kiwi fruit are a few examples. Ask him to guess what the objects are. He can collect some objects and give you a turn at guessing too.

MASSAGE CIRCLE

Three or more people sit on the floor in a circle facing each other's backs. Each person massages the back of the person in front of him. The more the merrier!

GROUP HUG

Stand in a circle facing each other and put your arms around each other for a group hug. This is particularly nice for families. If the children are very small lift them up and hold them in your arms during the hug or kneel down so you are all about the same height.

BLINDFOLD WALK

Materials: blindfold

Tell the child what you are going to do before you do it. She must feel secure and trust you to enjoy this game. Tie a clean scarf around her eyes to blindfold her. Turn her around three times. Lead her slowly to another room, then ask her to guess what room she is in. She will use her ears, nose, and sense of touch by listening for familiar noises, sniffing for familiar smells, and feeling the floor coverings with her feet, to discover where she is. Let her have a turn blindfolding, turning, and leading you to another room too.

MUMMY

Materials: roll of toilet paper, mirror, bag

Tell the child you are going to wrap him like a mummy and when you're finished he can break out of his wrapping by just lifting his arms and moving his legs. In front of a full-length mirror, starting at his shoulders, wrap him with a roll of toilet paper. Have him turn slowly as you guide the paper from the roll. Keep wrapping until you reach his ankles, then tear the paper off the roll and tuck it under at his ankles. If the paper tears off the roll while you are wrapping, just tuck it in and start from where you left off. Once he is completely wrapped, tell him to break out of his "mummy" wrapping by flailing his arms and dancing around. The paper will fall to the ground. Join him in squeezing golf- or tennis-size balls out of the toilet paper pieces on the floor. Toss the balls into a brown paper bag six to eight feet away or have a "snowball fight" with them. Save the paper balls in the bag for future games of "bag ball."

FOLLOW THE SOUND

Ask the child to wait in one room while you go into another to hide. Tell him to find you by listening for a sound you will be making every two seconds. Make a consistent sound like "la, la," or "tweet, tweet," or whistling every two seconds. When he finds you have him hide and make a sound to be found.

WHAT DO YOU SMELL?

Materials: blindfold, foods to smell

Ask the child to sit in a chair and tie a soft cloth blindfold around her eyes. Tell her you are going to put different foods close to her nose for her to smell and try to guess what each is. Foods like vanilla extract, garlic, herbs, vinegar, cinnamon, and mint candy work well. Don't use any foods like onions that might be too strong or unpleasant. If you use a piece of mint candy as the last food to guess you can end the game by placing the candy on her tongue.

TASTE TEST

Materials: blindfold, foods to taste

This game is similar to What Do You Smell? above except you let the child taste different foods. Foods like apple and orange slices, peanuts, raisins, potato chips, pretzels, a spoonful of ice cream or flavored yogurt all work well for this game.

X MARKS THE SPOT

This is one of many "tactile poems" children enjoy and love to memorize. It goes like this:

> X marks the spot
> with a dot, dot, dot,
> a line, line, line,
> and a question mark.
> A wiggle here, wiggle there,
> a little wiggle everywhere.
> Rain.
> Egg cracking.
> A cool breeze,
> and a warm squeeze.

While reciting the poem write an X on the child's back with your index finger, then make three dots, then draw three lines and a question mark. Wiggle your fingers in one place on her back, then another place, then all over her back. For the rain slowly and gently tap your fingers on her head. For the cracking egg touch her head with your fingers in a fist position, then slowly draw your fingers down from the top of her head. For the cool breeze give a gentle blow gently on the side or back of her neck. For the warm squeeze give her a gentle hug or a little squeeze on the arm or shoulder. She'll love doing the poem on you too.

EIGHT

CLAP YOUR HANDS, STAMP YOUR FEET
Music

In their preface to *Wee Sing*, Pamela Beall and Susan Nipp state, "Music can create a special closeness and joy to those who experience it together. However, for a child, there is more to music than mere enjoyment. Language development, muscular coordination, body awareness, rhythmic proficiency and auditory discrimination are a few of the benefits acquired from an early exposure to music. The young child is eager for musical and rhythmic experiences...."

Most of the songs in this chapter include movement (swaying, squatting, jumping, skipping, hopping, rocking, dancing, and clapping). The list of songs offered here is intended to spur you onto remember, sing, and act out your own favorite songs. If you want to add to your family's repertoire of songs, I highly recommend the *Wee Sing, Wee Sing and Play,* and *Wee Sing Silly Songs* series by Pamela Beall and Susan Nipp.

Some ideas for "instrumentals" are also presented in this chapter. They are great for playing duets, trios, quartets, or symphonies. Being part of the band makes taking turns, listening, imitating, and cooperating really worth the effort.

SINGING GAMES

This Little Light of Mine

Materials: flashlight or candle

Sing this song in a dark room or closet while holding flashlights. Try using candles (not in a closet) for a really special effect.

Row, Row, Row Your Boat

Sit on the floor cross-legged, facing each other. Hold hands and rock back and forth (this is rowing the boat) slowly at first, then faster and faster; slow down again for the end of the singing. Try singing it as a round.

Did You Ever See a Lassie

Take turns initiating and imitating movements when singing the "this way and that way" part of the song. Swaying, squatting, hopping, waving arms, kicking legs, and walking on your knees are a few ideas for this song.

Skip to My Lou

Skip as you sing the first verse, then take turns making up subsequent verses to run, walk, hop, jump, and slide to. You'll be surprised at the great verses children come up with.

Ring-Around-the-Rosy

Fall down for the first verse of this classic much-loved song but then try jumping up on the second verse, clapping hands on the third, clapping feet on the fourth, and so on.

Hokey Pokey

Kids still love this song. I'm just including it here so you don't forget about it. Take turns singing what will be "put in, out, and shaken about." You don't have to stick to the traditional lyrics; try putting in tongue, ear, finger, toe, knee, lips, and so on.

Found a Peanut

Materials: peanut

This is the traditional long song. Hide a peanut in an obvious place for the child to find. When he finds it break into song. Children learn this one very quickly. It can be done with a group by having a peanut for each child.

Old McDonald Had a Farm

Take turns naming the animals and making the sounds. Try looking like the animal you're singing about by making its beak, ears, tail, or wings with your hands or arms.

CLAPPING SONGS

Sit on the floor cross-legged, facing each other, and clap your thighs, hands, and your partners' hands while singing songs like "Miss Mary Mac," "Playmate," "Hambone," "Bingo," and "Once There Were Three Fishermen." The clapping action for many of these songs is described in the *Wee Sing and Play* book mentioned in this chapter's introduction.

ACTIVE SONGS

Sing and move to your favorite songs. Songs that I have found to be very popular with children are "If You're Happy and You Know It," "Here We Go 'Round the Mulberry Bush," "Put Your Finger in the Air," "Move, Move, Move," and "The Finger Band Has Come to Town." If you want to learn more songs, public libraries often have a good collection of children's records. Each of the songs above tells what movements to make either explicitly or by describing an activity to act out.

THE BODY AS AN INSTRUMENT

Sit on the floor facing each other, or in a circle if you have a group. Decide on a simple rhythm and then slap your thighs to the rhythm, then your knees, then hands. Next, slide and then stamp your feet. Now rub your hands together, then cluck your tongue. Can you or the children come up with any more instrumental body ideas?

KEYS

Materials: keys on a key ring

Keys can be used to keep time and accent music in the same way a tambourine is used. Have the child or children jingle the keys at appropriate times during a song. I once attended a concert where the audience was asked to use their keys as the bells for the song "Walking in a Winter Wonderland." It sounded quite impressive. You can listen to recorded music and play along with it as well as playing the keys while you sing.

HOMEMADE BAND

Materials: see each individual instrument below

Use one, two, or any combination of the following "instruments" to make music together.

maracas   Fill a mason or other jar with a tight-fitting lid with dry beans, peas, rice, or popcorn kernels. Shake the jar rhythmically.

string instrument   Wrap rubber bands (use different thicknesses if possible) around a shoe or other sturdy box. Strum and pluck the instrument.

comb kazoo   Wrap a piece of waxed paper around a comb and hum into it. You can play any tune on this versatile instrument.

drums   Empty oatmeal boxes, pots, boxes, or cookie tins make fine percussion instruments.

cymbals   Strike two flat pot covers together.

gong   Tie a string through a pot cover handle. While dangling the "gong" strike it with a wooden spoon.

triangle   Tie a string to a fork. Strike the dangling fork with another fork.

horn   Use a paper towel tube to hum and sing through. Cover and uncover the other end to muffle and change the sound.

washboard   Use thimbles on your fingers to strum the washboard. You can also use a wooden spoon to play this instrument.

tambourine   Shake a set of metal measuring spoons. They sound very much like a tambourine.

sandpaper blocks   Tack sandpaper to two blocks of wood. Rub together.

MARCHING BAND

Materials: instruments

Use any of the instruments you have made or have around the house. March around raising your knees high while singing and playing your instruments.

HARMONICAS

Materials: two harmonicas

Take turns imitating one another playing a short phrase on the harmonica. Play high, low, fast, slow, loud, soft, and so on. Then take turns listening to each other play a longer song. Try playing together, have one person play solo, then play together.

NAME THAT TUNE

Take turns humming a tune and guessing its title.

SCARF BUTTERFLY DANCE

Materials: two large scarves

Do this dance while singing or humming. Tell the child to pretend he is a caterpillar. He might crawl and slither on the ground. Put one folded scarf in each of his hands. Then tell him to huddle into a ball like a caterpillar in his cocoon who will soon be ready to come out as a beautiful butterfly. Tell him to slowly rise and let the scarves unfold as he dances with his butterfly wings flying all round.

NINE

LET'S DO IT TOGETHER

Cooperation

ooperation makes whatever you're doing twice the fun. The sum always ends up being more than its parts. When I think about children and cooperation I am reminded of a Richard Scarry story entitled "Pig Will and Pig Won't," in which Pig Will goes off with his father to help him at the boatyard. Pig Will works together busily with everyone at the boatyard and they all have a good time. He gets lots of special jobs to do and feels proud and responsible, and, of course, hungry hard workers deserve an ice cream break. Meanwhile, Pig Won't is bored at home. When he hears of all the fun Pig Will had, he changes his tune and becomes Pig Me Too!

The games and activities in this chapter illustrate the concept that you can't do alone what you can do together and that cooperation is just plain fun. Experiencing the fun of working together will foster a cooperative attitude in children.

PILLOW SONG AND DANCE

Materials: small throw pillows

Make up a song about shaking the pillows ("shake 'em high, shake 'em low, to the side, there they go...") while you raise them high, low, to the side, tap your thighs and knees, swing them between your legs, and put them on your own and each other's heads. When you finish your pillow song and dance pile them on top of each other to build a tower. This can be done by an adult and child or by two or more children.

COOPERATIVE PICTURE

Materials: paper and pencils, crayons, markers, paint and brushes

Take turns drawing features on a face (one draws a nose, the next a mouth, the next an ear, and so on), or take turns drawing parts of a body or animal, or details of a house or landscape. Use one or more of the above drawing implements. Be sure to sign both your names and display the picture. Try using pencils the first time you try this activity. Next time use crayons, the next markers, and so on. This can be done with an adult and child or two or more children.

COOPERATIVE SCULPTURE

Materials: self-hardening clay, small container of water

Take turns adding parts to a torso, person, animal, monster, or other object you decide to sculpt. Work on a formica or plastic surface if possible. Make silt (very gooey clay) for attaching parts. Carve your initials into the bottom. Let the sculpture air-dry for a few days to a week. To clean the work area, just wipe the surface with soapy water. This activity can be done by an adult and child or by two or more children.

DRAW EACH OTHER

Materials: timer, paper and pencils, crayons, markers, pens, paint and brushes

Sit at a table across from each other. Arrange your paper and whatever drawing implements you have decided to use. Set the timer for five or ten minutes and begin to draw one another. When the timer goes off sign your name and show each other your picture. Be sure to say only positive things about the child's picture of you. Make specific comments of praise about color, line, shapes, etc. Display your work. Use different drawing implements each time you try this activity. This can be done with an adult and child or two children.

DRAW A DESCRIBED PICTURE, THEN LOOK AND DRAW

Materials: paper, pencils, newspapers or magazines

Choose a photo of a person's face from a magazine or newspaper. Try to look for an interesting face (a man with a large nose or beard or wrinkles). Don't let the other person see the photo you have chosen. Take turns describing your photo to the other person while he draws from your description. When you have both had your turn show each other the photos you described. Now draw the face again while looking at the photo.

This is a truly fascinating exercise. It's amazing how many characteristics you can draw accurately from a description. You depend on each other for a view of a slice of life. This can be done by an adult and child or by two children.

BAG WALK

Materials: paper grocery bag, timer

Make sure you have a clear path down a hallway or from one side of the room to the other. Remove your shoes and place one foot (your right and the child's left or vise versa) into the paper bag. Walk across the room together. You will both have to move your feet forward at the same time to make any effective progress. Time yourselves and see if you can do it more quickly with practice. This can be done by an adult and child or by two children.

TIED-LEG WALK

Materials: scarf, timer

This is similar to Bag Walk above but you tie your right leg to the child's left leg and see how quickly you can walk together.

BALLOON WALK

Materials: balloon

Place a balloon between your tummies, backs, or foreheads and walk around a table without letting the balloon drop. If you make it all the way around, give each other a treat (candy, nuts, or raisins). If you drop the balloon keep trying until you succeed. This can be done with an adult and child or two children.

COTTON BALL RELAY

Materials: bag or bucket, cotton balls, timer

Place a bag or bucket of cotton balls at one end of the room and an empty bag or bucket at the other end. Set the timer for two minutes and take turns picking up one cotton ball at a time. Then, as quickly as you can, get to the other end of the room and deposit the ball into the empty bag or bucket. Then come back to where you started and tap your teammate's hand. Remember you are a team playing against the clock. See if you get faster with practice. Give yourselves a prize when you finish your teamwork. Can be played by two or more.

ROPE JUMP

Materials: jump rope

Stand facing each other and pretend to turn an imaginary rope while you both jump together. Then use a real rope in different ways. Turn the rope while you both jump together. Tie the rope to a fence or post and turn it while the child jumps. Then have her turn the rope while you jump. Swing the rope in a circle on the ground and have the child jump over it; then let her swing it for you to jump over. This can be done by an adult and child or by two or more children.

Speech bubble: TOUCH YOUR FINGERS, TOUCH YOUR TOES, BLINK YOUR EYES, WIGGLE YOUR NOSE... YEA, BUDDIES!

TENT TIME

Materials: four chairs, a blanket or sheet, a snack or game or pencils and paper

Build a tent together by draping the blanket over the chairs. Once inside, share a snack, play a game, draw each other, or do one of the quiet activities in this book.

SECRET GREETING

Make up a special parent-child secret greeting. Take turns suggesting things you'll do for your greeting (touch noses, wink, snort, hug, and so on). Add to it each time you do this activity until it is as long as you want it to be.

PLAY STORE

Materials: empty food containers, basket, bags, calculator, play or real money, shoe box

Kids love to play store with real merchandise. Save empty cereal boxes, juice cans, and other containers and store them in a big box. Whenever you want to play, drag out the box and stock the shelves together. If you don't have an empty bookcase, stock a table or counter. Put the basket and bags near the "cashier's station" (a table with the calculator and the shoe box with money). Once your store is set up (which is half the fun) take turns being the shopper; fill your basket and take it to the cashier who will calculate the price, bag it, and make change for your purchase. Then return the merchandise to the shelf and switch roles. When you're finished playing, become the store's stock personnel and return the containers to their big storage box.

TEN

ALL ABOARD

Rides

Everybody loves to go for a ride. The rides in this chapter, with the exception of the train and bus rides, involve either being ridden by the child or pulling, pushing, or swinging the child. You should be in good physical condition (no bad backs) before engaging in these activities.

Be sure you've got plenty of energy for the activity you choose. You wouldn't want to run out of gas right in the middle of a lot of fun. Be aware, however, that children often don't want to stop when they're really enjoying themselves. When you're tired out or feel enough time has been spent, take charge and say it's time to go onto the next fun you've planned. Don't use rides as the last activity in a play session. Remember it's always better to wind down with a calming activity and then an eating activity.

FOOT RIDE

Have the child take off his shoes and step onto the tops of your feet. Put your arms around each other and start walking forward, backward, sideways, with small and big steps, slowly, then quickly. It's also fun to dance and hum a tune together.

PIGGYBACK

We're all familiar with this old standby. Kneel down and let the child put his legs around your waist and his arms around your neck. Then stand up and prance around. A little bouncing is usually much appreciated. When you're finished with the ride kneel down and let him slide off.

KNEE RIDE

Sit in a chair and have the child straddle one knee facing you. Hold him by the waist or hands while bouncing the knee up and down. Singing a cowboy song like "I Ride an Old Paint" or "Ragtime Cowboy Joe" can add to the fun.

SHOULDER RIDE

Children love this ride because they get a giant's-eye view. We all know how much children want to be big. This ride gives them that big feeling. Crouch down and have the child put her legs over your shoulders. She should hold onto your head and you should hold the front of her calves. Stand up slowly and go for a walk with her perched on your shoulders. If you do this indoors make sure that all areas are high enough (no low doorways) so she won't hit her head.

AIRPLANE

Children love to be swung around but be sure to hold them under their arms and not by their arms to prevent pulling an arm out of its socket. Have the child face toward or away from you, whichever she finds most comfortable. Grasp her from under her arms, lift her, and spin around. To prevent getting dizzy, stop and swing her in the opposite direction. At the end of the flight, serve a small snack on a tray.

HORSEBACK

Get down on your hands and knees. Have the child climb onto your back and hold onto your shoulders. Now slowly walk on hands and knees and make a few horse-like noises as you amble along.

BLANKET SWING

Materials: blanket

This activity requires two adults. Lay a sturdy blanket on the ground and have the child lie down on it. Each adult lifts two corners of the blanket at the head and foot of the child. Now slowly swing him, first high, then low, a little faster, then very slow. Make up a song to sing while you swing.

TRAIN RIDE

Materials: chairs, paper, hole puncher

This works as well with three or four kids as one. Place a few chairs in a row to simulate a row of train seats. Issue a ticket to each rider (a piece of paper) and call out "All aboard." All riders should bounce around in their seats as if the train is moving. Playing the role of conductor, collect each ticket, punch it, and return it to the rider. Of course during this time you will be carrying on conductor-to-passenger conversations and calling out the different stops. When the tickets have been punched, make a whistle noise and switch off the lights to simulate the train going through a tunnel. When you've arrived at your destination let the child or each child take a turn at being conductor.

MAGIC CARPET

Materials: blanket

Lay a sturdy old blanket on the floor and ask the child to sit on it. Facing him, take hold of two corners and pull him as you walk backward. Tell him this is a magic carpet ride that can take him wherever he wants to go. When you arrive at the desired destination, tell the child this is the end of the line and to get off until you call out "All aboard." Then ask him to sit facing the opposite direction for the ride "home."

OFFICE-CHAIR RIDE

Materials: office chair on wheels

If you are lucky enough to have a chair on wheels available you can give great rides going backward, forward, sideways, even spinning around. Don't go too fast; keep your hands on the chair, guiding it at all times.

BUS RIDE

Materials: chairs, paper, hole puncher, coins, box

This is similar to Train Ride except that each person takes a turn at being the bus driver. The driver punches a hole in a transfer and hands it to each passenger that drops a coin in the box placed next to the driver. Once the passengers are seated, the driver steers the bus, steps on the gas and brake pedals, calls out street names, and answers passengers' questions. Set a timer if you have more than one child playing to ensure that each person gets his fair driving time.

ELEVEN

SLURP, SIP, DIP

Eating

Because eating is nurturing, calming, and rewarding, it provides the perfect closure to a play session. The food games in this chapter add another dimension to snack time—just plain fun! The activities are interactive; they involve feeding one another, guessing, using food as game pieces and then feeding each other the pieces, sharing food, or making and eating a snack together. Be sure to also provide a drink with the snack. Bon appétit!

FEED EACH OTHER

Materials: snack food

Simultaneously feed each other Popsicles, pretzels, crackers, or any other food. Hold a drink up for each other to sip from.

SSLLLURPPPPP!

SLURP TOGETHER

Materials: bowl, straws, yogurt or Jell-O

Put yogurt or Jell-O into a bowl. Sip it up through straws. Try to make as much slurping noise as possible.

FINGER DIP

Materials: pudding or yogurt, chopped nuts and/or raisins

Serve pudding or yogurt in a bowl without utensils. Dip fingers in the sticky pudding or yogurt and then in the bowl of nuts or raisins. Now lick off the delicious combination.

POPCORN TOSS

Materials: popcorn

Take turns tossing popcorn into each other's wide-open mouth.

TIC-TAC-TOE

Materials: pencil, paper, snack food

Use peanuts and raisins or other small snack food. Each person gets one kind of food for his playing pieces. On a clean sheet of paper, draw four lines for a tic-tac-toe game. Take turns placing the snack playing pieces in the squares. Winner eats all! Loser feeds the winner. If it's a tie, players feed each other. Be sure to let the child win at least one more time than you. Have enough snack food available for at least three to five games.

PRETZEL ON A POLE

Materials: small pretzels

Place a small pretzel on your little finger. Have the child bite off pieces from the "pole." Take your turn biting off pieces from the child's finger "pole."

NO-HANDS CHIPS

Materials: chips

Hold a potato or corn chip between your teeth. Have the child bite off a piece. You eat what is left. Now switch and bite off a piece of the chip she is holding between her teeth.

PUDDING, YOGURT, OR WHIPPED CREAM DRAWING

Materials: pudding, yogurt, or whipped cream, tray

Spoon pudding, yogurt, or whipped cream onto a tray; use it the same way you would use finger paint. Of course licking one's fingers during painting and before cleanup adds to the fun.

BANANA SHAKE

Materials: jar with lid, fork, cup of milk or orange juice, banana

Have all the ingredients ready and let her make you both a shake. Mash the banana with a fork. Put it in the jar, then add the milk or orange juice. Screw the lid on tightly and shake well. Pour into a glass and enjoy.

GUESS WHICH HAND
(EENIE MEENIE MINIE MOE)

Materials: treat

Hide a treat in one hand. Hold out both closed hands and ask the child to guess which hand holds the treat. Once she guesses which hand holds the treat, feed it to her. Try teaching her the traditional chant "Eenie meenie minie moe / Catch a tiger by the toe / If he hollers let him go / Eenie meenie minie moe." She should say one word while touching each hand alternately. The hand the chant ends on is the one she chooses. If she chooses the empty hand have her try again, this time starting at the opposite hand.

TASTE TEST

Materials: blindfold, snack food

Blindfold the child. Use fruits, nuts, chips, or other foods your child likes. Place the food on his tongue and ask him to guess what it is. He gets all the foods whether he guesses them or not.

ANTS ON A LOG

Materials: knife, celery, peanut butter, raisins

Spread peanut butter into the valley of a piece of celery. Top it off with raisins. Feed each other. It's moist, crunchy, sweet, and delicious.

FOOD SEARCH

Materials: snack food

Hide raisins, pieces of candy, pretzels, or other foods around the room or on yourself (in a pocket, sock, or up your sleeve). Let the child know when he's getting closer or farther to a hidden food by telling him he's getting "warmer, hot, cooler, or cold."

CHEESE BALLS

Materials: cream cheese, walnut pieces

Wash hands. Roll cream cheese into one large ball or any number of smaller balls. Then roll the ball or balls around in a plate of walnut pieces. Spread on crackers and eat.

FINGER LICK AND MUSTACHE

Materials: spoon, yogurt or peanut butter, raisins, whipped cream, mirror

Decorate the child's fingers with yogurt and raisins or peanut butter and raisins. Let her lick it off. Squirt canned whipped cream above the child's lip to make a mustache. Let him lick it off while watching in a mirror.

LIFESAVER ROD

Materials: Lifesavers, drinking straw

Place Lifesavers on the drinking straw and ask the child to bite them off. Have her refill the rod, then take your turn biting them off.

REFERENCES

Ayres, A. Jean, Ph.D., *Sensory Integration and the Child,* Western Psychological Services Publishers, Los Angeles, 1985.

Beall, Pamela Conn, and Nipp, Susan Hagen, *Wee Sing* and *Wee Sing and Play,* Price/Stern/Sloan Publishers, Inc., Los Angeles, 1981.

———. *Wee Sing Silly Songs,* Price/Stern/Sloan Publishers, Inc., Los Angeles, 1986.

Jennings, Sue, editor, *Creative Therapy*, Putnam, New York, 1975.

Jernberg, Ann, M., *Theraplay,* Jossey-Bass Publishers, San Francisco, Washington, London, 1983.

Oppenheim, Joanne, F., *Kids and Play,* Ballantine Books, New York, 1984.

Saunders, Antoinette, Ph.D., and Remsberg, Bonnie, *The Stress-Proof Child,* Holt, Rinehart and Winston, New York, 1984.

INDEX

rhythm, 86, 91
rhythmic proficiency, 86
Rides, 105–12
"Ring-Around-the-Rosy," 42, 88
ring toss, 10
rolling, 74
Rope Jump, 102
"Row, Row, Row Your Boat," 87

S
sandpaper blocks, 93
Scarf Butterfly Dance, 94
Screen Wash, 15
sculpture, 98
Secret Greeting, 103
Seed Spit, 18
self-awareness, 35, 60
self-confidence, 35, 54
self-esteem, 35, 38
senses, 73–84
sensory input, 74
Sensory Stimulation, 73–84
Shadow Trace, 21, 68
shaking hands, 71
sharing, 114–15, 117, 119, 121
Shaving-Cream Drawing, 27
Sheet Balloon Ball, 6
Shoe Switch, 64
Shoulder Ride, 108
sight, 74

Singing Games, 87
sizes, 32, 64, 70
"Skip to My Lou," 88
Slurp Together, 115
smell, 74, 80, 83
Snake Slither, 43
Snow Painting, 21
soccer, 4
singing, 86–90, 74, 94, 96, 107, 109
soothing, 114
sounds, 36, 62, 74, 82
spell, 51, 76
Spin the Bottle, 56
spitting, 18
Squirt, 14
string instrument, 92
sucking, 28, 63
surprise, 50
swinging, 74, 78, 106, 109

T
Taco, 77
tactile, 26–36, 79, 84
tambourine, 93
taste, 26, 33, 74, 83, 119
Taste Test, 83, 119
Telephone-Book Ball, 8
Tent Time, 103
tennis, 6
"This Little Light of Mine," 87
throwing, 3, 5, 7–10, 13, 116
Throwing and Ball

Games, 1–10
Tic-Tac-Toe, 116
tickling, 29, 41, 53, 76–77
Tickle Turns, 76
Tied-Leg Walk, 101
Towel or Sheet Balloon Ball, 6
Tower Knock, 45
tracing, 20–21, 67–69
Train Ride, 110
Tug-of-War, 46
turns, 50, 63, 76, 97–98, 100, 114–17, 119, 121

U
Unwrap, 57
V
volleyball, 6
W
"Walking in a Winter Wonderland," 91
washing, 14–16, 19, 29–30
washboard, 93
Water Balloons, 13
What Do You Smell?, 83
Wheelbarrow, 47
Window Wash, 16
Winter Indoor Sand Substitutes, 36
Wrestling, 47

X
X Marks the Spot, 84
Y
Yarn Spiderweb, 34

126